**Introductory**

# LANGUAGE
## Power

gagelearning

Editorial Team: Chelsea Donaldson, Carol Waldock
Cover Adaptation: Christine Dandurand

ISBN-13: **978-0-7715-1026-7**
ISBN-10: **0-7715-1026-8**

13 14 15  14 13 12
Printed and bound in the United States

# Table of Contents

## Unit 5 Capitalization and Punctuation

## Final Reviews

## Unit 6 Composition

■ **Read and follow the directions. Write the words that are in the dark boxes.**

1. Put an <u>X</u> above the doghouse.

_____

3. Put an <u>X</u> under the doghouse.

_____

2. Put an <u>X</u> on the doghouse.

_____

4. Put an <u>X</u> inside the doghouse.

_____

5. Put an <u>X</u> beside the doghouse on the left.

_____      _____

6. Put an <u>X</u> beside the doghouse on the right.

_____      _____

- **Read the sentences. Follow the directions.**

1. A fast horse runs down a wet street.
   Colour the horse **brown**. Colour the street **grey**.
   Colour the water on the street **blue**.

2. A little car has a flat tire. Colour the car
   **yellow**. Colour the tires **black**.

3. Two boats go down a river. Colour the boats
   **pink**. Colour the sails **blue**.

4. A long flag hangs from a big balloon.
   Colour the flag **red**. Colour the balloon **purple**.

5. A big tent is beside four tall trees. Colour
   the tent **orange**. Colour the trees **green**.

# Organizing Information

■ **Cross out the word that does not belong.**

1. red    blue    white    ~~turtle~~

2. jump    play    dog    run

3. elephant    Kim    Terry    Yoko

4. book    frog    pencil    paper

5. cat    fish    raccoon    sister

6. happy    popcorn    sad    angry

7. breakfast    lunch    candle    supper

8. milk    water    juice    mud

9. cry    doll    ball    game

10. above    under    blue    beside

■ **Read the words in the box. Write each word in the correct group.**

| | | | | |
|---|---|---|---|---|
| red | eat | Andy | blue | dance |
| Lupe | write | yellow | Dennis | green |
| skip | orange | sing | Yuri | |
| Gina | Vince | talk | pink | |

| **Colours** | **Names** | **Actions** |
|---|---|---|
| red | Andy | eat |
| | | |
| | | |
| | | |
| | | |
| | | |

■ **Write the missing capital letters.**

A ____ C ____ E ____ G

____ I ____ K ____ M

O ____ Q ____ S ____

U ____ W ____ Y ____

A B ____ ____ E F ____

____ I ____ ____ L ____ ____

O ____ ____ R S ____

____ ____ ____ X ____ Z

# Missing Small Letters

- **Write the missing small letters.**

a    _____    c    _____    e    _____    g

_____    i    _____    k    _____    m    _____

o    _____    q    _____    s    _____

u    _____    w    _____    y    _____

---

a    _____    _____    d    e    _____    g

_____    i    _____    _____    _____    n

o    _____    _____    r    _____    t

_____    v    _____    _____    _____    z

■ **Write the missing letters.**

A   B   C   D

_____

_____

_____

■ **Write the letter that comes next.**

1. S   T   U___

2. H   I   _____

3. B   C   _____

4. P   Q   _____

5. M   N   _____

6. K   L   _____

7. V   W   _____

8. E   F   _____

■ **Write the letter that comes in the middle.**

1. J   K   L

2. E   ___   G

3. Q   ___   S

4. F   ___   H

5. W   ___   Y

6. C   ___   E

7. T   ___   V

8. M   ___   O

■ **Write the letter that comes before.**

1. A   B   C

2. ___   T   U

3. ___   N   O

4. ___   X   Y

5. ___   J   K

6. ___   F   G

7. ___   L   M

8. ___   H   I

**Unit 1, Study Skills**

# Putting Words in ABC Order

■ **Write the words in ABC order.**

**1.** a b c d e f

<u>c</u>at    **bird**

<u>b</u>ird    **cat**

<u>d</u>og    **dog**

**4.** e f g h i j

<u>g</u>ive _____

<u>h</u>elp _____

<u>f</u>ind _____

**2.** i j k l m n

<u>k</u>now _____

<u>m</u>e _____

<u>li</u>ke _____

**5.** l m n o p q

<u>o</u>n _____

<u>l</u>eft _____

<u>n</u>ear _____

**3.** q r s t u v w x

<u>w</u>e _____

<u>sh</u>e _____

<u>t</u>hey _____

**6.** m n o p q r s

<u>r</u>ed _____

<u>o</u>ne _____

<u>n</u>ame _____

■ **Number the words in ABC order. Then write the words in the right order.**

| | | | | |
|---|---|---|---|---|
| **1.** | | | **5.** | |
| _2_ bat | **1.** _air_ | | ___ joke | **1.** ___ |
| _1_ air | **2.** _bat_ | | ___ lake | **2.** ___ |
| _3_ cat | **3.** _cat_ | | ___ king | **3.** ___ |
| **2.** | | | **6.** | |
| ___ top | **1.** ___ | | ___ neck | **1.** ___ |
| ___ sea | **2.** ___ | | ___ owl | **2.** ___ |
| ___ rock | **3.** ___ | | ___ mail | **3.** ___ |
| **3.** | | | **7.** | |
| ___ egg | **1.** ___ | | ___ well | **1.** ___ |
| ___ fish | **2.** ___ | | ___ us | **2.** ___ |
| ___ dog | **3.** ___ | | ___ very | **3.** ___ |
| **4.** | | | **8.** | |
| ___ hat | **1.** ___ | | ___ yes | **1.** ___ |
| ___ ice | **2.** ___ | | ___ zoo | **2.** ___ |
| ___ gate | **3.** ___ | | ___ X-ray | **3.** ___ |

**Unit 1, Study Skills**

- A **dictionary** is a book of words. The words in a dictionary are in ABC order.
- **Guide words** are at the top of every dictionary page.
- The guide word on the left is the first word on the dictionary page.
- The guide word on the right is the last word on the dictionary page.

  EXAMPLE: **baby / bed**

  **baby** ᵐᵐᵐᵐᵐᵐ     ᵐᵐᵐᵐᵐᵐᵐᵐᵐ

  ᵐᵐᵐᵐᵐᵐᵐ     **bed** ᵐᵐᵐᵐᵐᵐ

- **Use the dictionary page in the EXAMPLE to answer these questions.**

  **1.** What is the first word on the page? _____

  **2.** What is the last word on the page? _____

- **Choose the pair of guide words below that you would use to find each word.**

  | fit / fun     race / run     see / sit |
  | --- |

  **1.** sent   <u>   see / sit                    </u>

  **2.** flag _____

  **3.** room _____

  **4.** four _____

  **5.** ranch _____

  **6.** sheep _____

- A dictionary shows how to spell words.
- A dictionary tells what words mean.

---

**many**  a large number

**middle**  in between

**neighbour**  someone who lives in the next house

**new**  never used before

**noise**  a sound that is loud

**open**  not shut

**paw**  the foot of an animal

**return**  to go back

---

- **Use the dictionary words to answer the questions.**

1. What word means "in between"? _____

2. What word means "the foot of an animal"? _____

3. What word means "not shut"? _____

4. What word means "a sound that is loud"? _____

5. What word means "a large number"? _____

6. What word means "someone who lives in the next house"? _____

   _____

7. What does <u>return</u> mean? _____

8. What does <u>new</u> mean? _____

   _____

---

**Unit 1, Study Skills**

- Some words have more than one meaning.
    EXAMPLE: **pet**   1. animal kept as a friend
    2. to stroke
    Michelle has a **pet** turtle. (meaning 1)
    Meli loves to **pet** his new puppy. (meaning 2)

- **Read the meanings. Circle the first meaning. Draw a line under the second meaning.**

**cold**   1. not warm   2. a sickness of

the nose and throat

**tie**   1. to fasten together with string

2. a cloth worn around the neck

**wave**   1. moving water   2. to move the

hands back and forth as a greeting

- **Choose the correct word from above to complete each sentence. Write the number of the dictionary meaning that goes with each sentence.**

1. Please _____ **tie** _____ your shoelaces.   _1_

2. Carlos gave Dad a new _____ for his birthday.   _____

3. Leslie splashed in a big _____ at the beach.   _____

4. I always _____ to my friends in school.   _____

5. Put on a coat if you feel _____ .   _____

6. Leo had a _____ and missed school today.   _____

# Table of Contents

> ■ The table of contents is a list at the beginning of a book. It shows the titles and page numbers of what is in the book.

## Table of Contents

| | | | |
|---|---|---|---|
| All Kinds of Pets . . . . . . . 5 | | Dogs . . . . . . . . . . . . . 17 | |
| Choosing a Pet. . . . . . . 7 | | Cats. . . . . . . . . . . . . . 21 | |
| Feeding a Pet. . . . . . . . 9 | | Fish . . . . . . . . . . . . . 24 | |
| Exercising a Pet . . . . . . 15 | | Birds . . . . . . . . . . . . . 26 | |

■ **Answer these questions.**

1. What is this book about? _____

2. On what page can you read about cats? _____

3. On what page can you read about choosing a pet? _____

4. On what page can you read about exercising a pet? _____

5. What can you read about on page 24? _____

6. What can you read about on page 26? _____

7. How many kinds of pets can you read about? _____

8. On what page can you read about dogs? _____

9. What can you read about on page 21? _____

10. What can you read about on page 17? _____

                  **Unit 1, Study Skills**

■ **Look at each picture. Follow the directions given by your teacher.**

1.

■ **Find the word that does not belong. Cross it out.**

1. above     help     inside     under

2. older     younger     longer     jump

■ **Read the words in the box. Write each word in the correct group.**

| | | |
|---|---|---|
| sandals | earring | boots |
| shorts | shirt | necklace |
| sneakers | bracelet | dress |

**Clothes**                **Jewellery**                **Footwear**

_____        _____        _____

_____        _____        _____

_____        _____        _____

■ **Fill in the missing letters in ABC order.**

**1.** C   D  \_\_\_\_\_        **3.** Q  \_\_\_\_\_  S        **5.** m   n  \_\_\_\_\_

**2.** G   H  \_\_\_\_\_        **4.** a  \_\_\_\_\_  c        **6.** v  \_\_\_\_\_  x

- **Number the words in ABC order. Then write the words in the right order.**

1. __1__ almost    almost _____

     ____ peanut _____

     ____ hot _____

2. ____ zip _____

     ____ you _____

     ____ teach _____

3. ____ point _____

     ____ and _____

     ____ town _____

4. ____ track _____

     ____ voice _____

     ____ wear _____

- **Circle the word that would be on the same page as the guide words. Write the word.**

     **flash / keep**

1. joke    away    bark    sell    _____

2. barn    hard    dollar    eight    _____

3. lamp    vote    grow    next    _____

- **Use the dictionary words to answer the questions.**

> **orange**    a round fruit
>
> **poor**    without any money
>
> **spin**    turn quickly
>
> **tame**    not wild

1. What word means "without any money"? _____

2. What word is a fruit? _____

3. What does spin mean? _____

4. What does tame mean? _____

■ **Look at the picture. Follow the directions given by your teacher.**

■ **Read and follow the directions.**

**1.** Write <u>milk</u> to the right of the glass of milk.

**2.** Colour the peanut butter brown.

**3.** Colour the jam purple.

**4.** Draw a circle around the knife.

■ **Write the words from the box on the lines under <u>Foods</u> or <u>Kitchen Items</u>.**

| peanut butter | knife | plate | jam | bread | glass |
|---|---|---|---|---|---|

**Foods**                        **Kitchen Items**

_____      _____

_____      _____

_____      _____

- **Read the meanings. Write the number of the meaning that goes with each underlined word.**

> **bark** **1.** the sound a dog makes **2.** hard outside covering of a tree

_____ **1.** The <u>bark</u> of the tree was smooth.

_____ **2.** We heard the dog <u>bark</u>.

- **Answer the questions. Use the table of contents.**

Table of Contents

| | |
|---|---|
| All Children Like Toys . . . 4 | Dolls . . . . . . . . . . . . . . 15 |
| Balls . . . . . . . . . . . . . . . 6 | Cars . . . . . . . . . . . . . . 18 |
| Balloons . . . . . . . . . . . 8 | Games. . . . . . . . . . . . . 25 |
| Bicycles . . . . . . . . . . 13 | Toy Animals . . . . . . . . . 32 |

1. What is this book about? _____

2. On what page can you read about bicycles? _____

3. On what page can you read about toy animals?_____

4. What can you read about on page 6? _____

5. What can you read about on page 25? _____

- **Write each list of words in ABC order.**

| 1. | bake _____ | 2. | goat _____ |
|---|---|---|---|
| | dish _____ | | moon _____ |
| | face _____ | | pond _____ |
| | airplane _____ | | lake _____ |

**Unit 1, Study Skills**

# Words That Rhyme

- Words that end with the same sound are called **rhyming words**.

  EXAMPLES: boy — toy     dog — log     cat — sat

- **Find a rhyming word on the ducks.**
  **Write it on the line.**

dish
ring

door
ship

duck
hop

1. stop _____

2. sing _____

3. floor _____

4. fish _____

5. trip _____

6. truck _____

- **Finish each question. Use a rhyming word from the tree.**

  1. Did you ever see a goat

     wearing a _____ ?

  2. Did you ever see a bug

     as big as a _____ ?

  3. Did you ever see a bee

     get stuck in a _____ ?

  4. Did you ever see a fox

     carry a _____ ?

  5. Did you ever see a duck

     driving a _____ ?

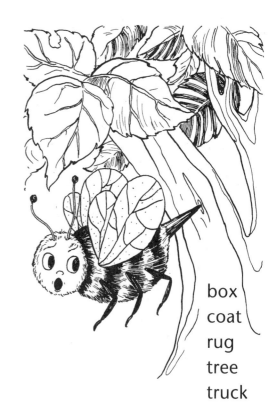

box
coat
rug
tree
truck

## Words That Mean the Same

- Words that mean almost the same thing are called **synonyms.**

grin — smile        sleep — rest

- **Circle the two words that are synonyms.**

1. sound    give    noise        3. all    every    one

2. high    down    tall          4. happy    sad    glad

- **Read the sentences. Circle the word that is a synonym of the underlined word.**

1. My book is on the <u>little</u> table.    (small, big)

2. It is a <u>large</u> book.    (red, big)

3. It is about a <u>rabbit</u>.    (dog, bunny)

4. My papers are <u>under</u> the book.    (on, below)

5. You can <u>print</u> in my book.    (see, write)

6. Now you can <u>stop</u> looking at it.    (finish, be)

7. I will <u>start</u> reading my book.    (be, begin)

8. I won't make a <u>sound</u>.    (noise, picture)

# More Words That Mean the Same

- **Circle a word in the second sentence that is a synonym of the underlined word. Write the two words on the lines.**

1. I hear a <u>sound</u>. The (noise) is my puppy.

   _____ sound _____     _____ noise _____

2. I <u>begin</u> to call his name. My puppy starts to bark.

   _____     _____

3. I <u>look</u> under the bed. I see him there.

   _____     _____

4. He is <u>glad</u> to see me. I am happy to see him, too.

   _____     _____

5. My puppy and I are <u>pals</u>. We will always be friends.

   _____     _____

6. Tiger is a <u>little</u> cat. He is small.

   _____     _____

7. Tiger heard a <u>sound</u>. It was a big noise.

   _____     _____

8. The cat ran <u>under</u> a tree. He was below a nest.

   _____     _____

9. A <u>big</u> bird looked down. The large bird chased Tiger.

   _____     _____

10. Tiger was <u>afraid</u>. He looked very scared.

    _____     _____

# Words That Mean the Opposite

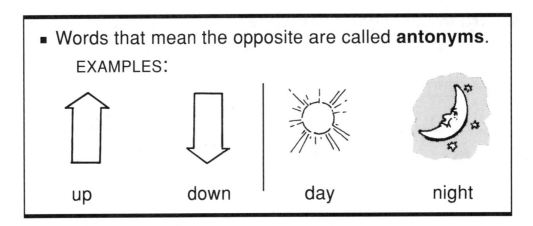

- Words that mean the opposite are called **antonyms**.

EXAMPLES:

up      down      day      night

- **Read the words. Connect the pictures that show antonyms.**

- **Read the sentences. Circle the word that is an antonym of the underlined word.**

1. Marco went <u>up</u> the stairs.   (down, out)

2. He sat on his <u>soft</u> bed.   (new, hard)

3. It got <u>dark</u> outside.   (light, cold)

4. He turned <u>on</u> the lamp.   (red, off)

**Unit 2, Vocabulary**

## More Words That Mean the Opposite

- **Read the sentences. Choose an antonym for the underlined word. Write both words on the lines.**

1. I am <u>little</u>, and my sister is _____ .

   _____little_____      _____big_____

2. She has <u>dark</u> hair, and I have _____ hair.

   _____      _____

3. When I go <u>out</u>, she comes _____ .

   _____      _____

4. Her bike is <u>old</u>, but mine is _____ .

   _____      _____

5. First I get <u>on</u> my bike, then I get _____ .

   _____      _____

6. I go <u>up</u> the steps and _____ the slide.

   _____      _____

7. I have a <u>hard</u> apple, and she has a _____ cookie.

   _____      _____

8. We play all <u>day</u> and sleep all _____ .

   _____      _____

9. The red tap is <u>hot</u> and the blue tap is _____ .

   _____      _____

10. My bag is <u>full</u>, but yours is _____ .

    _____      _____

> big
> cold
> down
> in
> light
> new
> night
> empty
> off
> soft

## Lesson 18 — Choosing the Right Meaning

- **Look at each pair of pictures. Read each sentence. Then write the letter of the correct meaning on the line.**

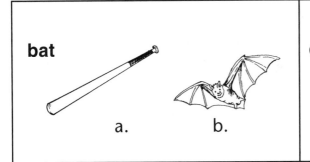

bat   a.   b.

duck   a.   b.

1. Steve hit the ball with a <u>bat</u>. _____

2. The <u>bat</u> likes the dark. _____

3. Juan plays ball with a heavy <u>bat</u>. _____

4. He wants to know how a <u>bat</u> sees at night. _____

5. I'd like a new glove and <u>bat</u>. _____

6. The <u>duck</u> made a loud quack. _____

7. There was a <u>duck</u> with four ducklings on the pond. _____

8. We had to <u>duck</u> under a fence. _____

9. We were asked to <u>duck</u> so they could see. _____

10. The <u>duck</u> swam in the water. _____

**Unit 2, Vocabulary**

# Writing Words That Sound Alike

> - Use **to** to mean "toward" or "to do something,"
>   EXAMPLE: Let's go to the library **to** find Kayla.
> - Use **two** to mean "the number 2."
>   EXAMPLE: **Two** children worked together.

- **Write to or two. Then write the whole sentence.**

1. I gave the ball _____ Ben.

   _____

2. Samantha went _____ the game.

   _____

3. There are _____ animals.

   _____

4. He wants _____ see.

   _____

5. I have _____ brothers.

   _____

- **Circle the correct word.**

1. I have (two, to) hands.
2. I use them (two, to) clap.
3. My house has (two, to) doors.
4. I open them (two, to) go outside.
5. I am going (two, to) the park.

© 1998 Gage Educational Publishing Company

■ **Circle the words that rhyme.**

| | | | | | | | |
|---|---|---|---|---|---|---|---|
| **1.** star | car | bat | | **5.** door | mouse | house | |
| **2.** log | hat | frog | | **6.** cat | hat | sit | |
| **3.** tug | rug | big | | **7.** ran | run | sun | |
| **4.** boat | goat | cap | | **8.** ants | pants | tin | |

■ **Draw lines to connect the antonyms.**

**1.** hard      down

**2.** up      new

**3.** old      soft

**4.** push      pull

**5.** in      dark

**6.** go      out

**7.** light      come

**8.** on      off

■ **Draw lines to connect the synonyms.**

**1.** little      big

**2.** stop      end

**3.** large      small

**4.** start      see

**5.** sound      begin

**6.** look      noise

**7.** print      under

**8.** below      write

Unit 2, Vocabulary

- **Write the letter of the correct meaning in the space.**

| pitcher  a.  b. | fly  a.  b. |
|---|---|

1. I will put milk in the <u>pitcher</u>. _____

2. The <u>pitcher</u> threw the ball. _____

3. The <u>pitcher</u> is almost empty. _____

4. I like to <u>fly</u> in a plane. _____

5. There is a <u>fly</u> on the window. _____

6. Can you <u>fly</u> a kite? _____

7. Can I be <u>pitcher</u>? _____

8. The <u>fly</u> buzzed in my ear. _____

- **Write <u>two</u> or <u>to</u> in the space.**

1. Ramona has _____ books.  (two, to)

2. She likes _____ read.  (two, to)

3. Her _____ friends like to read. (two, to)

4. They each took _____ books.  (two, to)

■ **Read the sentences. Write the word from the box that rhymes with the word below the line.**

| black | one | two | read | Funny | boy |

**1.** Kenji is the new _____ in class.
<u>toy</u>

**2.** He has _____ hair.
<u>sack</u>

**3.** Kenji likes to _____ books.
<u>seed</u>

**4.** He has read _____ books today.
<u>who</u>

**5.** He will read _____ tomorrow, too.
<u>fun</u>

**6.** _____ stories are Kenji's favourites.
<u>Sunny</u>

■ **Write two or to.**

**1.** I met _____ friends at the show.

**2.** We wanted _____ see something scary.

**3.** We bought _____ hot dogs.

**4.** We tried _____ find the best seats.

**5.** There were _____ bats in the show.

**Unit 2, Vocabulary**

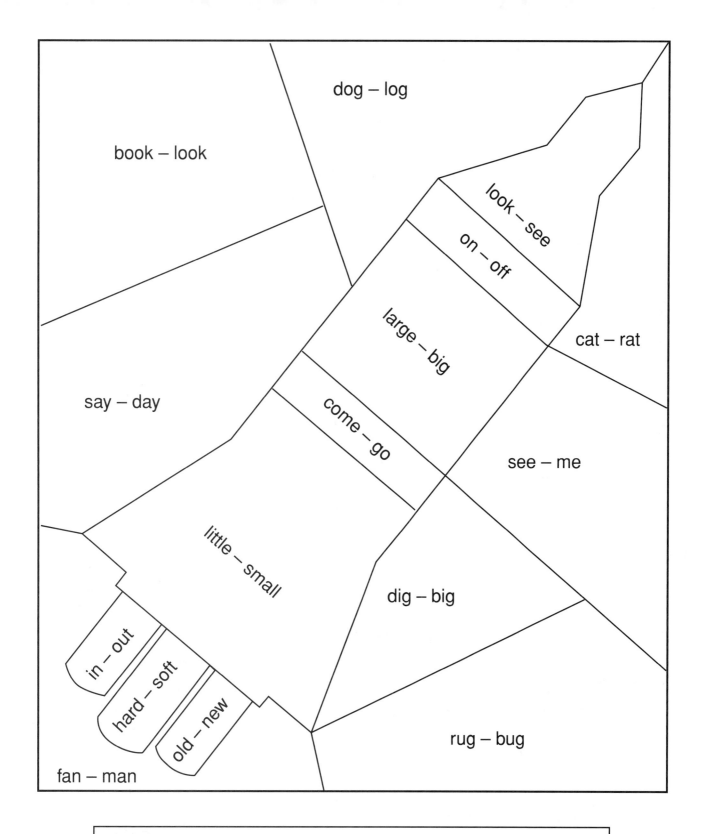

dog – log

book – look

look – see

on – off

large – big

say – day

come – go

cat – rat

see – me

little – small

dig – big

in – out

hard – soft

old – new

fan – man

rug – bug

Colour **antonyms** orange.  Colour **rhyming words** blue.
Colour **synonyms** yellow.

> ■ A **sentence** is a group of words that tells or asks
> something. It stands for a complete thought.
>     EXAMPLES: Friends play.   Cars go fast.

■ **Write <u>yes</u> if the group of words is a sentence.**
**Write <u>no</u> if the group of words is not a sentence.**

1. ___no___  A long time ago.

2. _____  The class went to the park.

3. _____  Near the tree.

4. _____  Ten children played.

5. _____  Maria hit the ball.

6. _____  A dog chased the ball.

7. _____  Bill and Tom.

■ **Read the sentences. Then fill in the blanks to**
**make another sentence of your own.**

1. Jan lost a new red shoe.

    Jan __played a game__ .

2. The sun was too hot for us.

    The sun _____ .

3. Some people sang songs.

    Some people _____ .

■ **Draw lines between the groups of words to make sentences. Then read the sentences.**

1. Mrs. Singh            live in our building.

2. Our building          is made of wood.

3. Four families         lives on my street.

4. Our school           was climbing the tree.

5. Jennifer             went on a picnic.

6. The sun              shone all day.

7. Corn and beans        fed the baby goat.

8. The wagon            has a broken wheel.

9. The mother goat        grow on a farm.

10. The boat            sailed in strong winds.

11. The fisher           were sold in the store.

12. Some of the fish      caught seven fish.

■ **Write a sentence about your birthday.**

_____

_____

■ **Write a sentence about your house or apartment.**

_____

_____

> ■ Words in a sentence must be in an order that makes sense.
>
>   EXAMPLES: Grandpa plays baseball.
>   My sister writes stories.

■ **Write these words in an order that makes sense.**

1. brother My apples eats

   <u>My brother eats apples.</u>

2. drinks Elizabeth milk

   _____

3. butter peanut Karla likes

   _____

4. Justin bread wants

   _____

5. corn plants Chris

   _____

6. a fish Chang caught

   _____

7. breakfast cooks Dad

   _____

8. his shares Shawn lunch

   _____

9. the Erica grew carrot

   _____

> ■ Sentences with <u>not</u> are called **negative sentences**. They tell about something that does not happen or is not true.
>
> EXAMPLES: Grandpa does <u>not</u> play baseball.
> Samantha can<u>not</u> ride a bike.

■ **Circle the number of each negative sentence. Underline the word <u>not</u>.**

**1.** John does not have a pet.

**2.** He has asked his mother for a dog.

**3.** John's mother will not let him have a dog.

**4.** John cannot get the pet he wants.

**5.** His mother may let him have a hamster.

**6.** Hamsters do not need to be walked.

■ **Rewrite each of the telling sentences as a negative sentence.**

**1.** I can find my key.

_____

**2.** Stan will go to school today.

_____

**3.** Kirin will bring his friend.

_____

**4.** They have finished their homework.

_____

> ■ A **telling sentence** is a group of words that tells something.
>
>    EXAMPLES: I fed my pony.
>    Ponies like to run and play.

■ **Write telling on the line before the group of words
if it is a telling sentence. Leave the line blank if
it is not a sentence.**

telling _____  **1.** Josh loves his pony.

_____  **2.** His name is Zip.

_____  **3.** Fast horses.

_____  **4.** He eats apples.

_____  **5.** Over the hill.

_____  **6.** Zip runs to Josh.

■ **Copy the telling sentences above.**

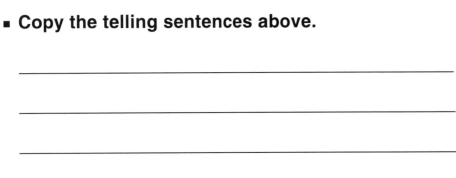

_____

_____

_____

_____

_____

Unit 3, Sentences

- An **asking sentence** is a group of words that asks a question. You can answer an asking sentence.
  EXAMPLES: How old are you?  Where do you live?

- **Write <u>asking</u> on the line before the group of words if it is an asking sentence. Leave the line blank if the group of words is not a sentence.**

  _____asking_____  **1.** Is this your friend?

  _____  **2.** Where does she live?

  _____  **3.** She in town?

  _____  **4.** How was school today?

  _____  **5.** Music and art?

  _____  **6.** Do you want a snack?

  _____  **7.** Where are the apples?

- **Copy the asking sentences above.**

  _____

  _____

  _____

  _____

  _____

  _____

## Exclaiming Sentences

> ■ A sentence that shows strong feelings or surprise is called an **exclamation**. Use an **exclamation point** (!) at the end of these sentences.
>
> EXAMPLE: What a fast ride that was!

■ **Write an X on the line before the group of words if it is an exclaiming sentence. Leave the line blank if the group of words is not a sentence.**

_____ **1.** What a lovely day it is!

_____ **2.** Apple pie is my favourite dessert!

_____ **3.** Hates snow!

_____ **4.** How high the roller coaster goes!

_____ **5.** Afraid of heights!

_____ **6.** My pet snake has escaped!

_____ **7.** That carpet is moving!

■ **Copy the sentences above that show strong feelings or surprise.**

_____

_____

_____

_____

_____

_____

# Telling, Asking, or Exclaiming Sentences

- **Circle the number of each telling sentence.
  Put an X on the number of each asking sentence.
  Underline the number of each exclaiming sentence.**

  **1.** I see a kite.

  **2.** Is it for me?

  **3.** What a nice surprise this is!

  **4.** How easily it soars up to the sky!

  **5.** Can I hold the string?

  **6.** I can run fast.

  **7.** I did not see that pole.

  **8.** That pole really hurt my head!

  **9.** Did you catch the kite string?

  **10.** I am so glad the kite did not fly away!

# Naming Part of Sentences

> - The naming part of a sentence tells who or what the sentence is about.
>   EXAMPLES: **Three mice** run away.  **The cat** plays with a ball.

- **Read the sentences. Then write the answer to the question.**

1. Jean played in the park.

   Who did something?_____

2. Sammy Doh brought the paper.

   Who did something?_____

3. Some children planted a garden.

   Who did something?_____

4. Ms. Clark washed her windows.

   Who did something?_____

- **Circle the naming part of each sentence.**

1. (My family and ) live on a busy street.

2. Sarah Harper found a bird.

3. Ms. Jenkins drives very slowly.

4. Mr. Olson walks his dog.

5. Henry throws to his dog.

6. Mr. Byrne cuts his grass.

**Unit 3, Sentences**

# Lesson 29

## Action Part of Sentences

> ■ The action part of a sentence tells what someone or something does.
>
> EXAMPLES: Three mice **run away**.  The cat **plays with a ball**.

■ **Read the sentences. Then write the answers to the questions.**

1. Amy found a puppy.

   What did Amy do? _____

2. The puppy ate some food.

   What did the puppy do? _____

3. The puppy played with Amy.

   What did the puppy do? _____

4. Amy named the puppy Skip.

   What did Amy do? _____

■ **Circle the action part of each sentence.**

1. My family and I (live on a busy street).

2. Sarah Harper found a bird.

3. Ms. Jenkins drives very slowly.

4. Mr. Olson walks his dog.

5. Henry throws to his dog.

6. Mr. Byrne cuts his grass.

■ **Choose a naming part to complete each sentence.**

| Lions Birds A pig A cat My dog Zebras |
|---|

1. _____Lions_____ roar loudly.

2. _____ have black and white stripes.

3. _____ rolls in the mud.

4. _____ plays with a ball of yarn.

5. _____ chews its new bone.

6. _____ fly in the sky.

■ **Choose an action part to complete each sentence.**

| barks buzz fly hops moo quack |
|---|

1. Robins and blackbirds _____fly_____.

2. Yellow bees _____.

3. My little dog _____.

4. Mother Duck and her babies _____.

5. A rabbit with big feet _____.

6. All the cows on the farm _____.

■ **Write a sentence about an animal that you like.**
  **Circle the naming part. Underline the action part.**

_____

# Combining Sentences

> - Combine two short sentences that closely share an idea to make one sentence. Use a comma (,) with one of the connecting words <u>or</u>, <u>and</u>, or <u>but</u>.
>   EXAMPLES:
>
>   You can go now. ⟶ You can go now, **or** you
>   You can go later.    can go later.
>
>   The rain is gone. ⟶ The rain is gone, **and**
>   The sky is blue.    the sky is blue.
>
>   Babies can't talk. ⟶ Babies can't talk, **but**
>   They can cry.    they can cry.

- **Add a comma plus the connecting word in brackets to join the sentences.**

1. Jim caught the ball. He threw it back. (and)

   Jim caught the ball _,___ __and___ and he threw it back.

2. Matt likes pizza. He hates pepperoni. (but)

   Matt likes pizza _____ _____ he hates pepperoni.

3. You can have a cookie. You can have cake. (or)

   You can have a cookie _____ _____ you can have cake.

4. Selim told a joke. Marcus laughed. (and)

   Selim told a joke _____ _____ Marcus laughed.

5. Sue lost her bag. Mary found it. (but)

   Sue lost her bag _____ _____ Mary found it.

■ **Write S if the group of words is a sentence. Write N if the group of words is not a sentence.**

_____ **1.** A lizard.

_____ **2.** Reptiles are cold-blooded.

_____ **3.** Snakes do not have eyelids.

_____ **4.** Found in warm places.

■ **Draw lines between the groups of words to make sentences.**

**1.** Keegan and Amina          teaches them how to play.

**2.** The big game              is Saturday night.

**3.** Their coach               play on the same team.

**4.** The phone                 is calling from Toronto.

**5.** Our uncle                 rush to answer it.

**6.** Marta and Matt            rings.

■ **Write the words in an order that makes sense.**

**1.** I broccoli like do not

_____

**2.** together our bikes We ride

_____

**3.** I not will book lose my

_____

**4.** we climb Sometimes trees

_____

- **Write T for a telling sentence. Write A for an asking sentence. Write E for an exclaiming sentence.**

1. _____ Did you go to the store?

2. _____ What did you buy?

3. _____ I will buy a card for Dad.

4. _____ What a nice present for Mom!

5. _____ These eggs smell rotten!

6. _____ Grandma needs some rice.

7. _____ Aunt Julia wants some milk.

8. _____ Where is the fish?

9. _____ I hope I can carry everything.

10. _____ The bag is broken!

- **Complete the sentences. Choose the naming part or the action part that is needed.**

| Many children are good friends | Mandy walks his dog |
|---|---|

1. _____ do chores after school.

2. Mandy and Jeff _____.

3. _____ cleans her room.

4. Jeff _____.

■ **Read the paragraph. Then read the pairs of sentences. Circle the asking sentence. Copy each asking sentence.**

Jenna's class is having a special day. Jenna is asking a friend to come to school. The friend will tell about her job. Jenna must write some asking sentences for her friend.

**1.** What is your job?

I would like to fly an airplane, too.

_____

**2.** Some children take a train.

Why do you fly an airplane?

_____

**3.** Are you scared in the air?

I like to eat the food in an airplane.

_____

**4.** Grandpa can meet me at the airport.

Do people have fun on an airplane?

_____

**5.** How old must you be to fly an airplane?

The airport looks busy.

_____

**6.** Some other people help on the airplane.

Do you meet any important people?

_____

- **Make sentences that tell what the class learned about flying an airplane. Draw a line from a naming part to an action part. Be sure the sentences make sense.**

| Naming Part | Action Part |
|---|---|
| **1.** A big airport | are very big. |
| **2.** Many airplanes | flies the airplane. |
| **3.** The people on airplanes | is a busy place. |
| **4.** A pilot | wear seat belts. |
| **5.** Many airport workers | work very hard. |

- **Make one sentence by writing the two short sentences before and after the connecting words.**

**1.** A pilot came to visit. Jenna asked her questions.

_____ , and _____ .

**2.** I like to fly. I am afraid.

_____ , but _____ .

**3.** I can take a train. I can go by bus.

_____ , or _____ .

**4.** I may be a pilot. I may be a doctor.

_____ , or _____ .

**5.** Jane's airplane was full. Roman's was empty.

_____ , but _____ .

**6.** I wore a seatbelt. Max did, too.

_____ , and _____ .

**7.** Our airplane was big. Mario's was bigger.

_____ , but _____ .

■ A **noun** is a word that names a person, place, or thing. The words <u>a</u>, <u>an</u>, and <u>the</u> are clues that show a noun is near.

EXAMPLES: a **man**, the **yard**, an **elephant**

■ **Find the nouns, or naming words, below. Write the nouns on the lines.**

| | | | |
|---|---|---|---|
| apple | car | eat | hear |
| chair | girl | hot | tree |
| boy | gone | came | dirty |
| pen | up | rug | ever |

1. ___apple___

2. _____

3. _____

4. _____

5. _____

6. _____

7. _____

8. _____

■ **Draw lines under the two nouns in each sentence. Write the nouns on the lines.**

1. The girl eats an apple. _____

2. A bird flies to the tree. _____

3. A chair is by the desk. _____

4. A boy sits in the chair. _____

**Unit 4, Grammar and Usage**

*Lesson*

# 33 Special Naming Words

> ■ A noun is a word that names a person, place, or thing. A **proper noun** is a word that names a special person, place, or thing. A proper noun begins with a capital letter.
>
> EXAMPLES: **Noun**     **Proper Noun**
> girl         Karen Stone
> park        Stanley Park
> bread       Tasty Bread

■ **Find the proper nouns below. Write the proper nouns on the lines.**

| | | | |
|---|---|---|---|
| baseball | China | man | prince |
| City Hall | Toronto | robin | Bridge Road |
| Gabriel | Nova Scotia | children | Linda |
| Pat Green | village | store | game |

1. _City Hall_      5. _____

2. _____      6. _____

3. _____      7. _____

4. _____      8. _____

■ **Draw a line under the proper noun in each sentence. Write each proper noun on the line.**

1. I bought apples at the Market Basket. _____

2. The store is on Baker Street. _____

3. It is near Stone Library. _____

4. I gave an apple to Emily Fuller. _____

> ■ Add -s to most nouns to make them name more than one.     EXAMPLE: a book, four books

■ **Rewrite these nouns to make them name more than one.**

**1.** cap _____

**2.** chair _____

**3.** girl _____

**4.** tree _____

**5.** flag _____

**6.** boy _____

> ■ Add -es to nouns that end with -x, -ss, -ch, or -sh to make them name more than one.
>     EXAMPLES: fox, ten fox**es**     class, a few class**es**
>     branch, five branch**es**     bush, six bush**es**

■ **Rewrite these nouns to make them name more than one.**

**1.** lunch _____

**2.** dress _____

**3.** glass _____

**4.** dish _____

**5.** box _____

**6.** watch _____

> ■ A **verb** is a word that shows action. Verbs tell what a person, place, or thing does.
> EXAMPLES: dogs **play**    I **eat**    Pat **reads**

■ **Draw a line from each noun to the correct verb, or action word.**

| Nouns | Verbs |
|-------|-------|
| **1.** The boy | sing. |
| **2.** The baby | bark. |
| **3.** The birds | cries. |
| **4.** The dogs | reads. |

■ **Draw a line under the verb in each sentence. Then write the verb on the line.**

**1.** Eric <u>kicks</u> a football into the air.          kicks

**2.** The ball breaks the Wilsons' window.          _____

**3.** Eric runs inside his house.          _____

**4.** Mother talks to Eric about the window.          _____

**5.** Mother sends Eric to the Wilsons' house.          _____

**6.** Eric pays for the window.          _____

**7.** Eric shakes hands with the Wilsons.          _____

## Naming Word or Action Verb

- **Draw a line under the two nouns, or naming words, in each sentence. Then write both nouns on the lines.**

   **1.** Our <u>class</u> meets in this <u>room</u>. ___class___  ___room___

   **2.** Our teacher reads us stories. _____  _____

   **3.** Some stories are about elephants. _____  _____

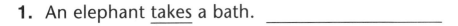

- **Draw a line under the verb, or action word, in each sentence. Then write the verb on the line.**

   **1.** An elephant <u>takes</u> a bath. _____

   **2.** The elephant sprays water with its trunk. _____

   **3.** The water cools the elephant. _____

- **Read the sentences. Write <u>noun</u> or <u>verb</u> for each underlined word.**

   **1.** Eddie and Susan <u>fly</u> their kites. _____

   **2.** The <u>kites</u> go up high. _____

   **3.** Eddie's kite <u>string</u> breaks. _____

   **4.** His kite <u>flies</u> away. _____

   **5.** <u>Susan</u> shares her kite with Eddie. _____

   **6.** Eddie <u>smiles</u> at his friend. _____

> - Verbs can tell about the action of one or more than one person, place, or thing.
>    EXAMPLES: One boy <u>plays</u>.    The toy <u>works</u> well.
>    Some boys <u>play</u>.    All the toys <u>work</u> well.

- **Underline the verb in each sentence. Circle the -s on the verbs that tell about one person, place, or thing.**

**1.** The dog <u>jumps</u>.
   The dogs <u>jump</u>.

**2.** The ball rolls slowly.
   The balls roll slowly.

**3.** The cat sleeps all day.
   The cats sleep all day.

**4.** My friend talks a lot.
   My friends talk a lot.

**5.** The apple falls from the tree.
   The apples fall from the tree.

**6.** My sister runs fast.
   My sisters run fast.

- **Write one of the underlined verbs above on each line.**

**1.** The girl _____jumps_____ rope.

   The girls _____ rope.

**2.** The orange _____ away.

   The oranges _____ away.

**3.** My pencil _____ on the floor.

   My pencils _____ on the floor.

**4.** My teacher _____ loudly.

   My teachers _____ loudly.

## Using *She* and *He*

> ■ Use <u>she</u> and <u>he</u> to take the place of people's names.
> EXAMPLES:
>
>
>
> **Jan** reads.   **Tony** writes.
> **She** reads.   **He** writes.

■ **Rewrite the sentences. Begin each one with <u>He</u> or <u>She</u>.**

**1.** Jan has a rabbit.

## She has a rabbit.

**2.** Tony has a fish.

_____

**3.** Jan pets the rabbit.

_____

**4.** Tony feeds the fish.

_____

**5.** Jan eats lunch.

_____

**6.** Tony eats lunch, too.

_____

**7.** Jan drinks milk.

_____

**8.** Tony drinks juice.

_____

**Unit 4, Grammar and Usage**

---

- Use <u>we</u> or <u>they</u> to take the place of more than one person's name.

  EXAMPLES:

  Tom and **I** will play.
  **We** will play.

  Lee, Pat, and Bill will play.
  **They** will play.

---

■ **Rewrite the sentences. Begin each one with <u>We</u> or <u>They</u>.**

1. Tom and I are here.

   ## We are here.

2. Lee, Pat, and Bill are not here.

   _____

3. Lee, Pat, and Bill are late.

   _____

4. Tom and I will play.

   _____

5. Tom and I can win.

   _____

6. Lee, Pat, and Bill will not play.

   _____

7. Lee, Pat, and Bill will be here soon.

   _____

8. Tom and I can wait.

   _____

---

- Use <u>an</u> before words that begin with a vowel sound.
  EXAMPLES: **an** apple, **an** egg
- The vowels are <u>a</u>, <u>e</u>, <u>i</u>, <u>o</u>, and <u>u</u>.
- Use <u>a</u> before words that begin with a consonant sound.
  EXAMPLES: **a** car, **a** skate

| | |
|---|---|
| a car | an apple |
| a rope | an egg |
| a skate | an iron |

- **Write <u>a</u> or <u>an</u>.**

1. _____ arm

2. _____ dog

3. _____ hat

4. _____ ant

5. _____ office

6. _____ fire

7. _____ cow

8. _____ can

9. Felix has _____ red bike.

10. Anu is _____ inch taller than me.

11. Stella sips _____ orange drink.

12. Randy put _____ apple in my box.

## Words That Describe Nouns

> ■ An **adjective** is a word that describes, or tells about, a
> noun. Adjectives tell which one, how many, or what kind.
>   EXAMPLES: the **muddy** boots    the **six** children
>   the **big** house

■ **Circle the describing word, or adjective, in each list.**

**1.** big, apple, eat, house

**2.** dog, cat, mouse, hard

**3.** he, she, neat, bed

**4.** shovel, snow, cold, nose

■ **Read the sentences. Circle the words that answer
the questions.**

**1.** Sally likes her new little rabbit.
It is brown and white and so soft.

Which words tell about Sally's rabbit?

red      white     little     new

brown   pretty    soft       wet

**2.** A little duck walked in the yard.
The duck was white and black.

Which words tell about the duck?

sad      white     dark       black

bad      little    lost       big

**3.** Joe lost his old brown cap.
Then he got two new red caps.

Which words tell about Joe's new caps?

old      brown     blue       lost

new      two       red        tall

## Words That Describe Verbs

> - An **adverb** is a word that describes, or tells about, a verb. Many adverbs end in <u>ly</u>.
>   EXAMPLES: Plants grow **slowly**.
>   The girl runs **quickly**.

■ **Circle the describing word, or adverb, in each sentence. Then write the adverb on the line.**

1. Gina laughed happily.

   _____

2. I whispered softly to my friend.

   _____

3. Walter awoke suddenly.

   _____

4. The tiger growled fiercely.

   _____

■ **Choose an adverb from the box to complete each sentence.**

| sleepily | loudly | softly | brightly |

1. The alarm clock rang _____.

2. I rubbed my eyes _____.

3. The sun shone _____.

4. My cat purred _____.

- **Circle the two nouns in each sentence. Draw a line under the verb in each sentence.**

    1. The children play on the beach.

    2. The sand hurts their feet.

    3. Boats float on the waves.

- **Write each proper noun on the line.**

    1. Mr. Harper is our teacher. _____

    2. We live in New Brunswick. _____

    3. My house is on Grenier Drive. _____

- **Add -s or -es to each word in ( ). Write the word on the line.**

    1. They wore _____ to the party.
       (dress)

    2. The _____ hold many things.
       (box)

    3. Four children played under the _____ .
       (tree)

- **Write the correct word in ( ).**

    1. This is _____ big farm.
       (a, an)

    2. The lambs _____ and play.
       (run, runs)

    3. The farmer has _____ old cow.
       (a, an)

    4. One cat _____ inside.
       (play, plays)

■ **Rewrite the sentences. Use a word from the box to take the place of the underlined words.**

| He   She   We   They |

1. <u>Rosa and I</u> went to a movie.

_____

2. <u>Maria and Dave</u> said it was a good movie.

_____

3. <u>Maria</u> wants to see it again.

_____

4. <u>Dave</u> wants to go again next week.

_____

■ **Circle the two adjectives in each sentence.**

1. The little lost kitten mewed at me.
2. Will's bag is blue and brown.
3. Two leaves fell from the old tree.
4. The big dog ate the hard bone.

■ **Write an adverb ending in <u>ly</u> to complete each sentence.**

1. Jim sat up _____.
2. Mario sews _____.
3. My dad wakes up _____.
4. Alanna looked at me _____.

| suddenly |
| sadly |
| early |
| carefully |

■ **Write a proper noun for each noun, or naming word.**
**Begin each proper noun with a capital letter.**

| Noun | Proper Noun |
|------|-------------|
| **1.** street | Elm Street |
| **2.** city | _____ |
| **3.** boy | _____ |
| **4.** girl | _____ |
| **5.** river | _____ |
| **6.** school | _____ |
| **7.** teacher | _____ |

■ **Complete each sentence with a describing word**
**(adjective or adverb).**

**1.** The star twinkled _____ in the sky.

**2.** The _____ dog followed the children home.

**3.** My eyes are _____.

**4.** Joe ran _____ to get help.

**5.** There are _____ people in my family.

■ **Write the correct word on the line.**

1. Tim and Maya _____ to play in the park.
   (love, loves)

2. Tim _____ quickly.
   (walk, walks)

3. Maya _____ slowly.
   (walk, walks)

4. Sam and I sometimes _____ our friends by the slide.
   (meet, meets)

5. Sam and I _____ turns on the slide.
   (take, takes)

6. Maya _____ to dig in the sandbox.
   (like, likes)

7. Tim _____ on the monkey bars.
   (climb, climbs)

■ **Copy four of the above sentences. Use He, She, We, or They to replace the underlined words.**

1. _____

2. _____

3. _____

4. _____

   **Unit 4, Grammar and Usage**

## Lesson
# 43

> ■ Each word of a person's name begins with a **capital letter**. EXAMPLE: **M**ary **A**nn **M**iller  **S**tuart **L**ittle

■ **Rewrite the names. Use capital letters where they are needed.**

**1.** dennis lee   Dennis Lee _____

**2.** roberta bondar _____

**3.** david suzuki _____

**4.** michael jordan _____

**5.** laura stern _____

> ■ Names of streets, parks, lakes, rivers, and schools begin with a capital letter.
> EXAMPLES:  **F**irst **S**treet
> **R**ed **R**iver
> **R**iverside **P**ark

■ **Rewrite the sentences. Use capital letters where they are needed.**

**1.** Shanti lives on market street.

_____

**2.** I think thomas park is in this town.

_____

**3.** We went to bellwood lake for a picnic.

_____

**4.** Is seton school far away?

_____

# Lesson 44

## Writing Titles of Respect

> - Begin a title of respect with a capital letter.
> - End <u>Mr.</u>, <u>Mrs.</u>, <u>Ms.</u>, and <u>Dr.</u> with a period.
>   EXAMPLES: **Mr.** George Selden   **Dr.** Alice Dahl
> - Do not end <u>Miss</u> with a period.

■ **Rewrite the names correctly.**

1. ms ruth pappas _____

2. mr kurt olsen _____

3. miss garcia _____

4. dr seuss _____

5. ms carol baylor _____

6. mr and mrs chin _____

7. miss jones _____

■ **Rewrite the sentences correctly.**

1. mrs stone is here to see dr milano.

   _____

2. dr milano and ms miller are not here.

   _____

3. miss loreto and mr lee arrived together.

   _____

4. mr green will go in first.

   _____

**Unit 5, Capitalization and Punctuation**

# Writing Names of Days and Holidays

> - Names of days of the week begin with a capital letter.
>   EXAMPLES: **M**onday    **F**riday

| Sunday | Monday | Tuesday | Wednesday | Thursday | Friday | Saturday |
|--------|--------|---------|-----------|----------|--------|----------|
|        |        | 1       | 2         | 3        | 4      | 5        |
| 6      | 7      | 8       | 9         | 10       | 11     | 12       |

■ **Write the days to complete each sentence.**

1. The first day of the week is _____ .

2. The day that comes before Saturday is _____ .

3. The day in the middle of the week is _____ .

4. I like _____ best.

> - Each word in the name of a holiday begins with a
>   capital letter.  EXAMPLES: **V**alentine's **D**ay   **L**abour **D**ay

■ **Write the holiday names correctly.**

1. new year's day _____

2. mother's day _____

3. canada day _____

4. remembrance day _____

5. victoria day _____

6. thanksgiving day _____

- Names of the months begin with a capital letter.
  EXAMPLES: **J**anuary   **D**ecember

■ **Write the months of the year correctly.**

1. january    _____ .

2. february    _____ .

3. march    _____ .

4. april    _____ .

5. may    _____ .

6. june    _____ .

7. july    _____ .

8. august    _____ .

9. september    _____ .

10. october    _____ .

11. november    _____ .

12. december    _____ .

■ **Write the month to complete each sentence.**

1. Valentine's Day is in _____ .

2. My birthday is in _____ .

3. The school year starts in _____ .

4. The last month of the year is _____ .

Unit 5, Capitalization and Punctuation

## Lesson 47    Beginning Sentences

> ■ Begin a sentence with a capital letter.
> EXAMPLE: **N**ow Deb and Jet play together.

■ **Rewrite these sentences. Begin them with a capital letter.**

**1.** deb likes to play ball.

_____

**2.** her ball is red.

_____

**3.** jet wants to play.

_____

**4.** jet likes the ball.

_____

**5.** deb throws the ball.

_____

**6.** the ball goes far.

_____

**7.** jet runs to the ball.

_____

**8.** jet brings the ball back.

_____

**9.** deb hugs her dog.

_____

**10.** they have fun together.

_____

## Lesson
# 48
## Ending Sentences

- Put a period (.) at the end of a telling sentence.
  EXAMPLE: Patty is my friend.
- Put a question mark (?) at the end of an asking sentence. EXAMPLE: Is she your sister?

■ **Rewrite these sentences. Use capital letters to start the sentences. Use a period or a question mark to end the sentences.**

**1.** helma plays on the baseball team

_____

**2.** is she a good player

_____

**3.** she hit two home runs

_____

- Put an exclamation point (!) at the end of a sentence that shows surprise or strong feeling.
  EXAMPLES: Watch out!     I am so excited!

■ **Rewrite these exclaiming sentences. Use capital letters and exclamation points.**

**1.** what a sad day this is

_____

**2.** that dog just bit me

_____

**3.** how tasty that meal looks

_____

© 1998 Gage Educational Publishing Company **Unit 5, Capitalization and Punctuation**

> ■ Use a comma to separate three or more items in a list.
>
> EXAMPLE: We took pencils, paper, and books to school.

■ **Put commas where they are needed.**

1. We go to school on Monday Tuesday Wednesday Thursday and Friday.

2. We draw sing and read on Monday.

3. Our class went to the post office the firehouse and the police station.

4. We ran jumped laughed and ate at the park.

5. Rachel John and Petra got lost.

■ **Rewrite the sentences. Use commas where needed.**

1. Pam Kay and Juan work hard.

   _____

2. Pam sings dances and acts in the play.

   _____

3. Kay cleans fixes and paints the stage.

   _____

4. Juan designs writes and prints the program.

   _____

## Using Commas in Place Names

> - Names of cities and provinces begin with a capital letter.
> - Put a comma between the name of a city and its province.  EXAMPLES:
>     Regina, Saskatchewan
>     Toronto, Ontario

■ **Write the cities and provinces correctly.**

1. halifax nova scotia  Halifax, Nova Scotia

2. montréal québec _____

3. ottawa ontario _____

4. edmonton alberta _____

5. nelson british columbia _____

■ **Rewrite the sentences. Use capital letters and commas where they are needed.**

1. Nancy lives in whitehorse yukon.

_____

2. Mr. Wong went to carstairs alberta.

_____

3. Did Bruce like winnipeg manitoba?

_____

4. Will Amy visit moncton new brunswick?

_____

5. How far away is happy valley newfoundland?

_____

         **Unit 5, Capitalization and Punctuation**

> ■ Put a comma between the day of the month and the year. EXAMPLE: January 1, 2000

■ **Write these dates correctly. Use commas where they are needed.**

**1.** December 12 1948 _____

**2.** March 27 1965 _____

**3.** September 8 1994 _____

**4.** November 1 1999 _____

**5.** January 5 2095 _____

■ **Complete the sentences. Write the date correctly on the line. Put commas where they are needed.**

**1.** Jim was born on _____ .
(August 10 1967)

**2.** Yanika's birth date is _____ .
(October 17 1991)

**3.** Maria visited on _____ .
(February 8 1996)

**4.** Dad's party was on _____ .
(July 29 1997)

**5.** Carrie starts school on _____ .
(September 3 1995)

**6.** My library books go back on _____ .
(March 17 1999)

**7.** I was born on _____ .

---

■ **Circle the letters that should be capital letters.**

1. selina has a turtle named speedy.

2. our two cats are named tippy and mittens.

3. david has a rabbit named fluff.

4. raffi and jessica play with fluff.

■ **Write the sentences correctly.**

1. mr bell did not work on friday

   _____

2. june is warmer than january

   _____

3. is thanksgiving in october

   _____

4. was ms smith going to be in the earth day parade

   _____

5. dr namis will be away on monday

   _____

■ **Rewrite the place names correctly.**

1. fifth street _____

2. red river road _____

3. mohawk drive _____

**■ Write these dates correctly.**

**1.** july 4 1990 _____

**2.** september 5 1991 _____

**3.** january 20 1993 _____

**4.** april 1 1994 _____

**5.** may 15 2001 _____

**6.** february 13 2020 _____

**■ Rewrite the sentences. Put commas where they are needed.**

**1.** Trina jumped ran and swam to win first place.

_____

**2.** The seasons are winter spring summer and fall.

_____

**3.** Dionne lives in Red Deer Alberta.

_____

**4.** This letter is going to Brandon Manitoba.

_____

**5.** Dana Maria and Natasha live in Fredericton New Brunswick.

_____

**6.** I used bread butter jam and peanut butter to make my lunch.

_____

■ **Everyone in the list below went on a trip. Imagine where and when each person might have gone. Draw a line from each person's name to the name of a place and then to a date. Then make a sentence about each person's trip. Be sure to use capital letters and punctuation correctly.**

| | | | |
|---|---|---|---|
| **1.** | dr yee | stone park | october 12 1994 |
| **2.** | jasmine | algonquin park | july 24 1996 |
| **3.** | mr hall | sunny beach | june 14 1995 |
| **4.** | miss greenberg | canada's wonderland | may 30 1996 |
| **5.** | becky | lake louise | september 2 1992 |
| **6.** | david | sea world | april 12 1995 |

1. <u>Dr. Yee went to Algonquin Park on September 2, 1992.</u>

2. _____

3. _____

4. _____

5. _____

6. _____

 **Unit 5, Capitalization and Punctuation**

# ■ Answer these questions about yourself.

1. What is your name?

   My name is _____.

2. What city and province do you live in?

   I live in _____.

3. Name the people in your family.

   The people in my family are _____.

4. Name two of your friends.

   My friends are _____.

5. What two holidays do you like best?

   I like _____.

6. What three months do you like best?

   I like _____.

7. What are four things you like to eat?

   I like to eat _____.

8. What are three things you like to do after school?

   After school I like to _____.

9. Where do you like to go on Saturdays?

   On Saturdays I like to go _____.

- A **paragraph** is a group of sentences about one main idea.
- The first line of a paragraph is **indented**. There is a space before the first word.

    EXAMPLE:

    Fluffy is my cat. She is four years old. She is black and white. She likes to play with yarn. She likes napping in the sun.

■ **Read the paragraphs. Answer the questions.**

Charise is studying for her math test. The test is on Friday. She wants to get a good grade on the test. She knows that studying will help her do well on the test.

**1.** Who is this paragraph about? _____

**2.** Write the first sentence of the paragraph.

_____

Today is my sister's birthday. She is five years old. She is having a party. Six of her friends are coming to the party. They will eat cake and play games.

**1.** What is this paragraph about? _____

_____

**2.** Write the first sentence of the paragraph. _____

_____

- The beginning sentence of a paragraph tells the **main idea**. It tells what the paragraph is about.
- The other sentences in a paragraph give **details** about the main idea in the beginning sentence.
  EXAMPLE:

  **I have nice neighbours**. Ms. Hill gives me flowers. Mr. Stone always smiles and waves. Miss Higgins plays ball with me.

- **Read the paragraphs. Circle the beginning sentences. Underline the sentences that give details about the main idea.**

Uncle Joe is a funny man. He tells jokes about elephants. He does magic tricks that don't work. He makes funny faces when he tells stories. He always makes me laugh.

TIGER!

Dad told us a funny story about his dog. When Dad was a little boy, he had a dog named Tiger. One day Dad forgot his lunch. Dad said Tiger would bring it to school. A friend thought it would be a real tiger.

- The **date** tells when the letter was written.
- The **greeting** tells who will get the letter. The greeting begins with a capital letter and ends with a comma.
- The **body** tells what the letter is about.
- The **closing** says goodbye. It begins with a capital letter and ends with a comma.

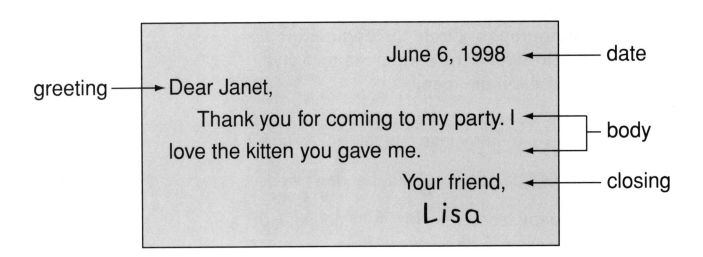

greeting

June 6, 1998 ← date

Dear Janet,

Thank you for coming to my party. I love the kitten you gave me. ← body

Your friend, ← closing

Lisa

- **Read the sentences. Write the words.**

   **1.** The date of the letter is _____ .

   **2.** The letter is to _____ .

   **3.** The greeting of the letter is _____ .

   **4.** The closing of the letter is _____ .

■ **Read the thank-you letter. Write today's date on the first blank line. Then copy the letter. Sign your own name on the last line.**

> May 1, 1998
>
> Dear Zookeeper,
>     Thank you for the book you sent our class. It was a very good animal story.
>
>                     Yours truly,
>                     Sara

today's date ⟶ _____

_____

_____

_____

_____

_____

your name ⟶ _____

■ **Read each paragraph. Circle the sentence that gives the main idea. Underline the sentences that give details about the main idea.**

1.     I really want a dog. I will take care of it. I will feed it every day. I will take it out for walks. I will give it baths. I will name it Scooter.

2.     Bob and Sue know how to cook. First, they read the recipe. Then they gather the things they need. Next, they mix them together. Finally, they put the dish in the oven.

3.     Firefighters are brave people. They go into burning buildings. They put out fires. They teach families to be safe in their homes.

- **Label the parts of the letter.**

| A. Body | B. Closing | C. Date | D. Greeting |
|---------|-----------|---------|-------------|

May 1999    **1.** _____

**2.** _____ Dear Uncle Kevin,

Thank you for taking me to the circus.

**3.** _____ I had a good time.

Love,

Kendra    **4.** _____

- **Fill in the missing parts of the letter. Use today's date and sign your own name.**

_____

_____ Lee,

Thank you for coming to my sleepover. I

had a good time.

_____,

_____

■ **Draw a line from the main idea to three sentences that give details about the main idea.**

| Main Idea | Details |
|---|---|

**1.** I take care of my teeth.

I brush after every meal.

I visit the dentist.

My jacket is warm.

I floss my teeth.

**2.** Summer is my favourite season.

We went skating last winter.

The sun is hot.

We can play all day.

We can go to the beach.

**3.** I have a new bike.

It has a red seat.

My brother does not know how to ride a two-wheeler.

It goes very fast.

It has a horn.

**4.** Janice is sick.

She is my best friend.

She has a fever.

She has been coughing and sneezing.

The doctor told her to rest.

**Unit 6, Composition**

- **Write a thank-you letter to someone in your class.**

- **Write today's date on the first line.**

- **Write <u>Dear</u> _____ in the greeting.**

- **In the body, write
  Thank you for coming to my
  party. I had fun.**

- **Write a closing that you like.**

- **Write your name below the closing.**

_____

_____

_____

_____

_____

_____

_____

- **Check your spelling. Check to see that you used
  commas and capital letters where needed.**

**Following Directions** ▪ **Look at the picture. Follow the directions given by your teacher. Then follow the directions that are written below.**

**1.** Colour the rocks brown.

**2.** Colour the castle blue.

**3.** Circle the snail on the wall.

**4.** Put an <u>X</u> on the fish in the castle.

**Organizing Information** ▪ **Cross out the word that does not belong.**

**1.** eye    flag    ear    nose

**2.** bark    farmer    teacher    banker

**3.** dog    cat    horse    flower

**4.** blue    book    red    yellow

**Missing Letters** ▪ **Write the missing letters.**

1. A    ___    C    4. f    g    ___

2. J    K    ___    5. m    ___    o

3. ___    Q    R    6. ___    x    y

    **Unit 1, Study Skills**

**ABC Order** ■ **Number the words in ABC order. Then write the words in ABC order.**

1. _____ chair          _____

   _____ hot            _____

   _____ angry          _____

2. _____ nest           _____

   _____ penny          _____

   _____ off            _____

**Guide Words** ■ **Underline the words that would be on the same page as the guide words.**

   **old / sea**

1. toast    poor    village    quack

2. nest    really    tonight    pair

**Using a Dictionary** ■ **Use the dictionary words to answer the questions.**

| **baby** a very young child | **broken** 1. not working |
| **birthday** the day someone was born | 2. in many pieces |

1. What word has two meanings? _____

2. What word means "a very young child"? _____

3. What does <u>birthday</u> mean? _____

**Table of Contents** ■ **Answer the questions about the table of contents shown below.**

| Table of Contents | |
|---|---|
| Why Forts and Castles Were Built . . 5 | Types of Castles . . . . . . . . . . . . . 23 |
| Types of Forts . . . . . . . . . . . . . 12 | Famous Forts and Castles . . . . . 34 |

1. What is this book about? _____

2. On what page can you read about types of forts? _____

3. On what page can you read about famous forts and castles? _____

**Rhyming Words** ▪ Circle the words that rhyme.

1. The cat sat on the mat.

2. The bug is on the rug.

3. The frog will hop on the mop.

4. The brown bear ate a pear.

5. A bee is in the tree.

6. I have fun when I run in the sun.

7. Jim took a ride down the slide.

8. Sue left her coat on the boat.

9. Pat likes to skate by the gate.

10. Is there a mouse in Pat's house?

**Synonyms and Antonyms** ▪ Draw a line under the correct word to complete each sentence.

1. Happy means almost the same as (sad, glad).

2. Sick means almost the same as (well, ill).

3. Yell means almost the same as (smile, shout).

4. Laugh means almost the same as (giggle, cry).

5. The opposite of clean is (dirty, old).

6. The opposite of quick is (slow, fast).

7. The opposite of easy is (simple, hard).

8. The opposite of over is (under, above).

**Words With Two Meanings** ▪ Look at each pair of
pictures. Read each sentence. Then write the letter
of the correct meaning on the line.

**cook**  a.

**1.** _____  The restaurant is looking for a new cook.

**2.** _____  Mom will cook dinner for one hour.

**3.** _____  Juan wants to be a cook when he gets older.

**4.** _____  Your aunt is a wonderful cook!

**fly**  a.

**5.** _____  My uncle will fly to Europe.

**6.** _____  Would you like to fly in an airplane?

**7.** _____  That fly keeps buzzing by my ear.

**8.** _____  The frog ate the fly.

**play**  a.   b.

**9.** _____  Our class will put on a play next week.

**10.** _____  My friend and I like to play together.

**11.** _____  What game would you like to play?

**12.** _____  Scott wants to play football.

---

**Sentences** ▪ Write <u>yes</u> if the group of words is a sentence.
Write <u>no</u> if the group of words is not a sentence.

_____ **1.** Look at the plants.          _____ **4.** Came from the sky.

_____ **2.** Six tiny beans.          _____ **5.** The plants will grow.

_____ **3.** It is raining.          _____ **6.** The sunshine will.

**Sentence Order** ▪ Write these words in an order that
makes sense.

**1.** was table Milk the on

_____.

**2.** from Butter comes milk

_____.

**3.** Cheese milk also comes from

_____.

**4.** Joanna to drink like does not milk

_____.

**5.** spilled his milk Brad

_____.

**Telling, Asking, or Exclaiming Sentences** ▪ Write <u>T</u> for telling sentences.
Write <u>A</u> for asking sentences. Write <u>E</u> for exclaiming sentences.

**1.** _____ Is Mom home from work?          **5.** _____ He went to the library.

**2.** _____ She has to work late.          **6.** _____ Why did he go to the

**3.** _____ What a clean room!          library?

**4.** _____ Where did Dad go?          **7.** _____ He wants to check out a

**Naming Part of Sentences** ▪ Choose a naming part to complete each sentence.

| Phillip        My family        Katie and Kathy |
|---|

1. _____works together to clean the house.

2. _____ dusts the bookshelves in his room.

3. _____do the laundry.

**Action Part of Sentences** ▪ Choose an action part to complete each sentence.

| smells sour        tastes sweet        feels rough |
|---|

1. The orange _____.

2. A lemon _____.

3. The sandpaper _____.

**Sentence Parts** ▪ Circle the naming part of each sentence. Draw a line under the action part of each sentence.

1. Our class surprised Miss Muller.

2. All the children brought flowers.

3. Sarah and Shawn put them in a glass.

**Combining Sentences** ▪ Use a comma plus the joining word in ( ) to join the two sentences into one sentence.

1. Sher's hat is blue. Her coat is red. (and)

   Sher's hat is blue _____ _____ her coat is red.

2. The sun is hot. The wind is cold. (but)

   The sun is hot _____ _____ the wind is cold.

3. We can go now. We can go later. (or)

   We can go now _____ _____ we can go later.

**Naming Words and Action Words** ▪ Circle the naming words. Underline the action words.

**1.** Dad walked to the store.

**2.** Mom rode the bus to Royal City.

**3.** John plays in the park.

**4.** Lee jumped rope.

**Using We, They, She, and He** ▪ Rewrite the sentences using We, They, She, or He.

**1.** Brad and I went bowling.

_____

**2.** Shelly and Jared met us there.

_____

**3.** Shelly got a strike.

_____

**4.** Brad won the game!

_____

**5.** Shelly, Brad, and I needed to leave.

_____

**6.** Jared said goodbye to us.

_____

    **Unit 4, Grammar and Usage**

## Using A or An ▪ Write A or An in front of the words.

1. _____ boat

2. _____ apple

3. _____ bus

4. _____ egg

5. _____ door

6. _____ uncle

## Words That Describe Nouns ▪ Circle the describing words.

1. The small otter likes to play.

2. The otter is brown.

3. It swims in the cool water.

4. It has a warm coat.

5. The otter is happy.

## Words That Describe Verbs ▪ Circle the words that describe verbs.

1. Pina tiptoed quietly into the room.

2. The candle burned brightly in the window.

3. The tree swayed gently in the wind.

4. The music played softly in the background.

5. The snow fell thickly on the ground.

**Capitalization** ▪ Circle the letters that should be capital letters.

1. mr. sanchez works at harris school.

2. mr. kelly took his class to riverside park.

3. they will go to the columbia river in september.

4. will sasha come to see reza?

5. did bill come on tuesday?

6. donna took a boat ride on lake erie last week.

7. donna and i met ms. slade last monday.

8. we went to a party for mrs. lee in november.

**Holidays** ▪ Complete the sentences. Use capital letters where needed.

| | |
|---|---|
| new year's day   (January) | thanksgiving   (October) |
| canada day   (July) | st. valentine's day   (February) |
| victoria day   (May) | labour day   (September) |

1. On July 1, Canadians celebrate _____ .

2. On _____ we give each other cards.

3. January 1 is _____ .

4. The school year begins right after _____ .

5. On _____ we celebrate Queen Victoria's birthday.

6. We eat turkey on _____ .

**Punctuation** ■ **Write the sentences correctly. Put periods, question marks, exclamation points, and commas where needed.**

1. What will you do in Banff Alberta

   _____

2. Who is with Dr Trigo

   _____

3. It is Mr Casey

   _____

4. What a surprise to see him

   _____

5. He likes to read dance and sing

   _____

6. His family moved there on June 4 1978

   _____

7. I will be out of town in March April and May

   _____

8. Did Ms Kirkpatrick go to Halifax Nova Scotia

   _____

9. Watch out for that car

   _____

10. Dr Nguyen will be in town on November 12

    _____

11. How can we get to Moose Jaw Saskatchewan

    _____

12. Miss Hall will be late on Monday Wednesday and Friday

    _____

**Paragraphs** ▪ **Read the paragraphs. Circle the sentence that gives the main idea. Underline the sentences that give details about the main idea.**

1.  Baseball is a sport I like very much. I like to play on the city team in the summer. I have been saving baseball cards since I was five. I like to watch games at night. I have a great time at the ballpark.

2.  Puppies like a lot of playtime. They like to chase balls. They play with people, as well as other dogs. They can play for hours.

3.  Kayla had an accident on her bike. She was riding in the park. Her front wheel stuck in a grate. The bike stopped, but Kayla kept going. She scraped both her knees. Luckily, she was wearing a helmet.

**Parts of a Letter** ▪ Write the labels next to the parts of the letter.

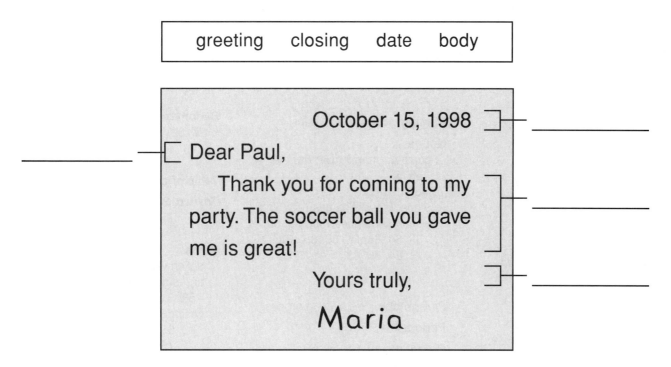

| greeting | closing | date | body |

October 15, 1998 ⌐ ————————

⌐ Dear Paul,
————

Thank you for coming to my
party. The soccer ball you gave
me is great!

Yours truly, ————————

Maria

**Thank-You Letter** ▪ Fill in the missing parts of the letter. Use today's date and your own name.

————————

———— Ali,
Thank you for finding our cat.
We were happy to get it back.

————————

————————

# Index

**A/an,** 52, 55, 87

**Action words.** *See* Verbs.

**Adjectives** (words that describe nouns)**,** 53, 56, 57, 87

**Adverbs** (words that describe verbs)**,** 54, 56, 57, 87

**Alphabet,** 4, 5, 6, 7, 8, 13, 14, 16, 80, 81

**Antonyms** (opposite words)**,** 20, 21, 24, 27, 82

**Capitalization**
  days of the week, 61, 68, 88
  first words of sentences, 63, 68, 88
  holidays, 61, 68, 88
  in letters, 74, 75, 77, 79, 91
  months of the year, 62, 68, 69, 70, 88
  names of people, 59, 60, 65, 68, 70, 88
  names of pets, 63, 68
  names of places, 59, 65, 68, 70, 88
  titles of respect, 60, 70

**Classifying,** 3, 13, 15, 80

**Commas,** 65, 66, 67, 69, 70, 89

**Dates,** 67, 69, 70, 74, 75, 77, 79, 89, 91

**Dictionary,**
  definitions, 10, 11, 14, 16, 81
  guide words, 9, 14, 81

**Exclamation points,** 34, 64, 89

**Following directions,** 1, 2, 13, 15, 80

**Homographs.** *See* Multiple meanings.

**Homonyms.** *See* To/two.

**Letters,** 74, 75, 77, 79, 91

**Multiple meanings,** 22, 25, 83

**Naming words.** *See* Nouns.

**Nouns**
  common (naming words), 44, 48, 55, 57, 86
  plural, 46, 55
  proper (special names), 45, 55, 57
  writing sentences with, 59, 60, 63, 64, 65, 66, 68, 69, 70, 72, 75, 84, 86, 88

**Paragraphs.** *See* Writing process.

**Periods,** 64, 67, 89

**Pronouns,** 50, 51, 56, 58, 86

**Punctuation.** *See* specific punctuation marks.

**Question marks,** 64, 89

**Rhyming words,** 17, 24, 26, 27, 82

**Sentences**
  action part (predicate), 37, 38, 43, 85
  asking, 33, 35, 41, 42, 64, 84
  combining part, 39, 43, 85
  exclaiming, 34, 35, 41, 64, 84
  naming part (subject), 36, 38, 43, 85
  negative, 31, 40, 68
  recognizing, 28, 29, 30, 32, 33, 34, 40, 84
  telling, 32, 35, 41, 64, 84
  word order in, 30, 40, 84
  writing exercises, 28, 29, 30, 31, 32, 33, 34, 36, 37, 38, 40, 41, 42, 43, 50, 51, 56, 58, 59, 60, 62, 63, 64, 65, 66, 68, 69, 70, 71, 72, 75, 77, 79, 84, 86, 89

**Sequence,** 4, 5, 6, 7, 8, 13, 14, 16, 80, 81

**Subjects**
  subject-verb agreement, 49, 55, 58

**Synonyms** (like words)**,** 18, 19, 24, 27, 82

**Table of contents,** 12, 16, 81

**To/two,** 23, 25, 26

**Verbs**
  action words, 47, 48, 49, 55, 86
  agreement with subject, 49, 55, 58
  writing sentences with, 37, 59, 60, 63, 64, 65, 66, 68, 69, 70, 72, 75, 84, 86

**Writing process**
  letter writing, 74, 75, 77, 79, 91
  paragraphs, 72, 73, 76, 90
  sentences, 28, 29, 38, 58, 70, 71, 79